Introduction

Not long ago, after an unusually productive business trip, I returned to my office with a tall stack of work. Upon eyeing and then picking up the stack, a colleague asked, "What's this @#x!%?" I responded, "It may be @#$!x to you, but it's bread and butter to me."

This is a book of business bread and butter.

My colleague soon thereafter left the organization. He should have known better. In this book, I have continued my attempt, begun in my first book, *Never Confuse a Memo with Reality*, to capture the conventional and not so conventional wisdom that people in business should know—but either ignore or never learned in the first place.

No one was more surprised than I by the success of my first book, *Never Confuse a Memo with Reality*. I believe it met several needs. First, it represents what many people know is the truth about life in today's organizations. Second, it is accessible: It features no complex models or theories that make anyone feel guilty or inadequate for not understanding. Third, the lessons from the book apply. No matter what their level, industry, or position, people understand. Fourth, there is humor in the book that makes people chuckle about their own situations. And, lastly, the price is right.

I wrote *Beware Those Who Ask for Feedback* always keeping in mind what readers told me about what they liked about *Never Confuse....*

If the "bullets" listed here help you better understand the current world of complex organizations and how to navigate through that world, then I have communicated well. If, after reading this book, you are more satisfied with your job and life, then I have been wildly successful.

Rich Moran

1. Always tell the truth to employees and your boss. It's easier to remember what you said.

2. Never buy a toy, piece of software, or computer game that features piercing electronic noises.

3. Just because you're a supervisor doesn't mean you have a license to be a jerk.

4. Never make quotation marks in the air with your fingers.

5. Quick Hits and Low-Hanging Fruit are never as quick or as low as everyone believes.

6. When you hire a consultant, get the consultant jokes out of the way early. The consultant has probably heard them all already.

7. Beware those who ask for feedback. They are really asking for validation.

8. Anytime you go back to your hotel room, expect the maid to be cleaning it.

9. Don't put your company's name on a vanity license plate. You'll have to re-register the car if you get laid off.

10. Flattening the organization doesn't necessarily mean anything changes.

11. Be wary of those who call and say they have no agenda.

12. Create a personal "Board of Directors" to help you make career decisions.

13. Employees are best at implementing strategies, not setting them.

14. Periodically, such as monthly, prepare status reports. They are useful when the time comes for your performance reviews. Otherwise, no one looks at them.

15. If your span of control is bigger than your shoe size, your job as a manager is probably safe.

16. Learning when to say no may help your career more than always saying yes and not meeting expectations.

17. Spend as much time and attention on learning how to communicate well as you spend learning technical matters.

18. "It is difficult to get a man to understand something when his salary depends upon his not understanding it." Upton Sinclair

19. There is never one solution to any organizational problem. Choose the best from among difficult alternatives by using clear criteria.

20. Be more results-driven than methodology-driven.

21. When you oversleep, spend an extra minute in bed to develop a recovery plan.

22. On a bad-weather day when there is no work, either play in the snow and have fun with the kids—or try to work from home as best you can. Don't get uptight about things you can't control, such as the weather.

23. Trust your instincts. There is a reason other people value your experience. You should as well.

24. Assume that no one likes or wants to pay consultants. What consultants should do, however, is get things implemented. That may be worth whatever you pay them.

25. Sweeter than getting the job you've always dreamed of is having the freedom to turn it down.

26. When everyone in the company walks around carrying a calculator, it means employees believe an early-retirement plan is about to be announced.

27. Don't pick your teeth with the business card of the client who just gave it to you.

28. If you think you're smarter than your boss, never let on. Your boss knows anyway.

29. In your written work, say something meaningful in the first sentence.

30. Avoid these excuses:

- We don't have time. (Since we downsized.)

- We don't know how. (Because there's no training.)

- We tried that before. (Under TQM.)

- We don't have the data. (The systems don't work.)

- We're unique. (It's not true.)

31. Too much resistance to a new system or change probably means there's something wrong with it. Employees will usually act in the organization's best interest. Listen to them.

32. Always go after the 80 percent and don't worry about the remaining 20 percent, which is seldom worth the effort.

33. Memos with the heading "Expense Report Preparation" never reduce work or expenses and are always a source of jokes for employees.

34. Always check job applicants' references.

35. Distill each paragraph into one sentence. Include that sentence in the paragraph.

36. If someone asks you for the time, answer the question. Don't tell them how to build a watch.

37. If you have nothing to say, say nothing. You will command much more attention when you do have something to say.

38. When hosting a long meeting, schedule time for nature breaks. Participants will take them anyway.

39. Don't teach your children how to swim or drive. Enroll them in swimming lessons and driver's education. It will eliminate tears and tantrums.

40. When you see someone from work away from work, such as at the supermarket, don't act like you just saw your teacher while playing hooky. Say hello and be relaxed.

41. Sometimes it's easier to change banks and open a new account than it is to reconcile your checkbook, but try to avoid that situation.

42. Career counseling with your spouse or significant other is risky. If you're too direct, the perception can be that you're manipulative. If you're too permissive, it can appear that you don't care.

43. Doing a great job often means you'll get more work. Understand this and use it to your advantage.

44. If unimplemented corporate strategies were pennies, we'd all be rich.

45. If you're going to watch the movie on an airplane, rent the headphones.

46. Strategies always look and sound better when announced. Reality sets in the next day.

47. If God is in the details, sometimes you may also need an even higher authority to answer the question, "To what end are we doing all this?"

48. Keep a journal, but not one in which you begin each page with "Dear Diary." Use a simple notebook where you make entries when something significant, interesting, or surprising happens. Someday it will help you answer the question, "Where did all those years go?"

49. Don't gossip. Don't do things that make you a party to gossip or the subject of gossip.

50. Avoid "Long-Term Parking" at all costs.

51. If you're becoming good friends with the night custodian and you have a day job, you're working too hard.

52. "Empowered employees" is often an oxymoron. Set your expectations accordingly.

53. "The system will be down" is one of the few constants in organizations.

54. Customers don't care how you're organized. Spend time on what they do care about.

55. Most communications problems can be solved with proximity.

56. Performance evaluations reflect the organization's attitudes toward employees. Ones that start with attendance and punctuality tell people to show up on time, but not necessarily to perform.

57. Work gravitates to the most competent.

58. If you can avoid it, don't fly with your boss or your client. You don't want them to see you sleeping with your mouth hanging open.

59. "Low-hanging fruit" refers to easy changes for big returns. Usually, most of it turns out to have already been picked.

60. To truly learn all the nuances and secrets of travel, travel with an experienced traveler or do the same thing that everyone wearing a business suit and carrying an Atlas briefcase and Hartmann suit bag does.

61. Know what is meant by the big R and little r in reengineering.

62. Be prepared to lose anything that you put in the "seat pocket in front of you."

63. Expect that anything you lose on an airplane you will never see again.

64. Reading business and trade publications keeps you apprised of buzzwords and trends. Reading fiction keeps you balanced.

65. Table seating at business luncheons and dinners should be arranged in advance.

66. Eliminate annoying habits like cracking your knuckles, smacking your lips, belching and catching it in your mouth, licking your fingers, and the like.

67. "Touchy feely" is not a good label. If it's been assigned to you, start doing things that are more practical.

68. When someone says, "Don't worry, you're young, marketable, and willing to relocate," it's time to worry.

69. Just like athletes are attracted to winning teams, employees are attracted to winning departments.

70. Get people's attention occasionally by doing something out of character. Don't be 100 percent predictable.

71. Never confuse making people happy with what needs to be done.

72. The easiest way to derail a meeting is to ask a question that will require a lot of detail.

73. Employees who say, "I only get paid to think from the neck down," are in trouble.

74. Supervisors who say you only get paid to think from the neck down should be fired.

75. Make decisions based on what's best for the customer, not on internal rankings.

76. Always turn your computer on when you're in the office—even if all it shows are toasters flying by.

77. Project scopes are always better when narrowly defined.

78. During a presentation, never say, "I'll get into this in a lot more detail in a minute."

79. If you get fired, give yourself two days at most to feel sorry for yourself. Focus on your next job, not your last one.

80. Never wear a workout suit or sweat clothes when flying.

81. Employees give management more credit for being smart than it may deserve. If they sat in on a few management meetings, they would know the truth.

82. Most organizations and people have about the right number of people—they're just doing the wrong things.

83. Take jobs that have an inherent brand recognition—either in the title or in the organization.

84. Don't ask a computer system to do what you wouldn't ask the organization to do.

85. Read the company newsletter.

86. Hope is a required ingredient for success.

87. If you drop names, make sure the target knows who you are talking about.

88. Using macho sports or military metaphors usually means you've lost half of your audience.

89. Never start a presentation out by saying, "I know you can't read this, but . . . " or "Bear with me while I . . . "

90. If you think the plane is going to crash, keep your shoes on.

91. Remember: The Scarecrow from *The Wizard of Oz* really did have a brain. He will be the successful manager of the nineties.

92. If you're going to fail, do it fast—but have a recovery strategy.

93. Don't try to get even with the organization or the boss. No one will win, but you *will* lose.

94. Too much travel will make you crazy and unhealthy.

95. Progress is made when the choices that are presented are limited and clearly defined. Remember how you deal with your children. Go to bed, or take a bath and go to bed. Pick one.

96. Don't roll your eyes in meetings.

97. Employee turnover can have its virtues.

98. There is no relationship between morale and organizational success. Positive morale does, however, make showing up for work more enjoyable.

99. New hires should bring new perspectives, not the company line.

100. There are two ways to travel: first class and with children.

101. Benefits are almost always more important than features.

102. Once in a while, sit in a window seat and look out the window to renew your sense of wonder at how airplanes even leave the ground.

103. If work goals and criteria for success are not clear, everyone will guess.

104. If you talk on airplane phones, expect that everyone around you will be able to hear you, listen, and probably be annoyed.

105. Spend job-hunting time with people who can hire you.

106. The golden rule at work should be: Employees should feel a sense of reward and recognition equal to or greater than their contributions.

107. The grapevine is usually about 90 percent right.

108. Someday you will have to fly with children. Be gentle to those who are sitting next to you screaming while they color Barney coloring books.

109. Keep a running record of the good things you do throughout the year. Your boss will keep the record of the not-so-good things.

110. If you get a below-average rating for a reason unclear to you, change departments, change supervisors, or change jobs.

111. In evaluations, no matter how many numbers
there are and what each is supposed to mean
regarding competence, if your ranking is in the
middle, it means average.

112. No matter how thoughtful it may be, what
everyone looks for in their review is the salary-
increase percentage.

113. If you're a supervisor, fill out the review forms carefully and spend the time necessary to let people know how they are doing. However, don't overengineer the process and make it tedious for everyone. After the review, your charges should know how they're doing and what else needs to happen. They should not leave dazed and confused.

114. Read the audience. If they're not paying attention, change gears.

115. Put at least one game on your computer to get warmed up.

116. Never get caught with a game on your screen.

117. Use the same type of hardware and software that the rest of your office uses, even if it's not your favorite.

118. Never hire a friend.

119. Never go into a partnership with a friend.

120. When the outcome of a meeting is to have another meeting, it has been a lousy meeting.

121. When you interview someone who will be a colleague, two key questions are:

- Would I want to have dinner with this person (meaning are you willing to spend time with the person)?

- Would I introduce this person to my Mom (meaning are you proud to be affiliated with the person)?

122. Learn how to conduct an interview so that you get the information you want.

123. Reward yourself and truly savor success by upgrading on return flights.

124. Start with a rough draft as soon as possible and fill in the details as you go. You'll find the end product will be similar to the original intention.

125. To what end? is always a good question to ask at the beginning of a big project.

126. Use editors and critics. As defensive as we all get, they do help.

127. Learn what a collar stay is and use them.

128. The *Land's End* catalogue has dress shirts that virtually never wear out.

129. It's better to look bad than to smell bad.

130. Never give up on projects until they are implemented.

131. Use exclamation points in business writing or titles only if someone's life is in danger. Avoid labels such as "The you in marketing!"

132. The new résumé-scanning software looks for traits, not accomplishments. Write your résumé assuming that it will be screened in. Use words like "pioneered" and "initiated."

133. Employees have a need to vent. Let E-mail play the role or hire consultants to make sure employees get that opportunity.

134. Job hunting resembles a target. You are the dot in the middle. The people in the first circle are the ones that know you and like you, but are the least equipped or able to help you. The outside circles are the people who are friends of friends and connections. That's where the jobs are.

135. Two of the most dreaded words in the English language are "shuttle bus." If you know the shuttle is part of the routine, see if there is an alternative.

136. More schooling never hurts. It may not have the immediate pay-off you want but it's not going to hurt.

137. At some point during each day, lean back in your chair and ask yourself, "What am I doing; is it a high priority; and is it helping me reach my goals?"

138. Learn how to spell names that could be important—it's Procter; it's Andersen; it's Zale.

139. Don't pick your nose in your car, even if you're alone. Others do see you.

140. The goal is not to be busy. The goal is to contribute something of worth that will make you glow.

141. Don't confuse details or volume with results. Many times a 10-page proposal is better than a 150-page proposal.

142. Learn what these sayings mean:

- Outside the box.

- No cookie-cutter solution.

- Low-hanging fruit.

- Connect the dots.

- Deep yogurt.

143. As a group of employees once said, "For every system you create, we'll create an equal and opposite system." If employees don't like systems, those systems are almost impossible to implement.

144. Read your mail soon after you receive it.

145. Violent agreement often occurs in meetings. Know when it's happening so you can move on.

146. In business, you can't have it both ways so pick one.

147. Never use a cellular phone in a restaurant.

148. Beepers are for physicians and others who may have to deal with an emergency.

149. Cutting prices to get business rarely works—and often backfires.

150. The only difference between a good haircut and a bad haircut is two weeks. The question is, Can you endure the two weeks?

151. Answer personal mail that you receive.

152. Use phone mail as an effectiveness tool, not a source of guilt. Don't skip messages that make you feel like you haven't done something, and especially don't store them. The problem won't go away. Listen to the message, see what needs to be done, delete the message, and take care of the problem.

153. Don't fight with hotel service people. Relax, let them do their work, and tip them appropriately.

154. Worry about the big things, and the little things will fall into place.

155. If a performance measure is hard to understand, it's not a good one. Use ratios whenever possible in creating measures such as revenues per employee, staff resources compared to line resources, and the like.

156. One measure is usually not enough. Measures that form equations are the best, like $x/y - q/s = $ effectiveness.

157. If pushed into recommendations, it's best to create alternatives and let the client choose. Don't be afraid to let your own bias be known, but share the decision-making responsibility. Always share the blame.

158. Work plans are useful only if they're short and include names, times, and outcomes.

159. Don't give out your home number unless you want people to call you. If colleagues do call and it's not a good time, tell them so.

160. "Connect the dots" is a metaphor for linking the things that you do. Try it.

161. "Cycle time" is a term that applies to all jobs. Know what it means and do all you can to reduce your cycle time.

162. Benchmarking is not a class trip at the company's expense. It has a purpose and is a measurable activity. Don't make it soft.

163. Best practices are often confused with soft benchmarking. Know what the difference is.

164. Name your children as if they were going to be President of the United States.

165. Treat all major organizational initiatives like a product and launch them with all the sensing and customer focus of a product launch.

166. Once you decide what there is to decide, work on who decides.

167. Always play the good cop.

168. When leaving a message for someone on their phone mail, always leave your number, even if they know it.

169. It's rarely a good sign when you don't hear. No news is not good news in sales, consulting, or interviewing.

170. Don't get too excited when you're waiting for the outcome of an interview or a proposal. It will blow any negative news out of proportion. Don't get excited until you actually know.

171. Use your clients' products. Don't give a presentation to 3M on a Kodak overhead projector or rent a Ford to call on Chrysler or General Motors.

172. Talk about health problems only with your doctor.

173. Don't put anything in your briefcase that you don't want others to see.

174. Worry more about doing the right thing than being politically adept.

175. If you're going through a divorce, it's probably a good idea to tell your supervisor. You don't need to keep it a secret from others, but you shouldn't use it as an excuse either. Most people don't care if you're single or married. They just want you to be happy.

176. Don't spend a lot of time creating missions—ask your employees.

177. Let arguments at work die. It's usually not worth it.

178. If you feel yourself falling asleep in a meeting, do something to prevent others from noticing.

179. Always take notes on meetings. Never assume others will, even when they say they will.

180. If you don't send out holiday cards, at least once a year send your key contacts an announcement so everyone is current on your address, phone number, and what you're doing.

181. There are no such things as communications, turnover, or morale problems. They are symptoms of other problems—usually autocratic management. Don't try to fix the symptoms. Fix the problems.

182. When *Business Week* or *Fortune* announces a
management trend, learn as much as you can
about it. It will probably be around for a while.

183. Never be embarrassed about where you grew up, where you went to school, how you look, your name, or anything else that it's too late to fix. Be proud of who you are.

184. Have a professionally done black-and-white photo of yourself always ready for publicity and other uses. Never allow yourself to be put next to the wall in a panelled conference room while someone takes a bad photo of you.

185. When people you respect recommend books, read them.

186. When someone sends you an announcement about a new job or a promotion, and you know the person, send them a note of congratulations.

187. Give money to your alma mater(s), no matter how little the amount.

188. If you keep a radio in your office, tune it to an appropriate station. Rock-and-roll morning shows should be saved for getting ready for work and/or the car ride. Then you can laugh and have fun.

189. Don't steal. Taking office supplies home is stealing. Copying software without permission is stealing.

190. Go to trade shows but be realistic about their benefits, which are to stay up-to-date on products and to network. Learn who has the best parties and who is giving out the best souvenirs.

191. Most organizations struggle to have it both ways. When they realize they can't, they move forward.

192. Next steps from meetings must always be clear.

193. Don't hire only people who look and act like you. It will make for a less interesting and less effective group.

194. Don't finish other people's sentences, especially your boss's.

195. When a Total Quality initiative begins with a series of posters, it's probably an initiative in trouble.

196. Put your own voice on your phone-mail greeting. Make it a professional message with an upbeat tone.

197. If you're married, wear your wedding ring.

198. Use New Year's resolutions as a real way of setting goals.

199. The result of week-long executive retreats should be more than a one-line mission that doesn't apply to the organization.

200. If you don't have a client, find one—before you have to find a job.

201. Casey Stengel said some people make things happen, some people watch things happen, and some people say what happened. Be in the first category.

202. Most organizations overengineer their change initiatives.

203. The test of communications is whether or not employees know what's important.

204. If you meet in a resort area, give people time off so they can enjoy it. Don't go to Orlando or Steamboat Springs and stick people in windowless meeting rooms all day.

205. If you're a guest and you break something, don't even ask if you should replace it—just replace it.

206. Performance measures should be viewed like the instruments on a car. It's a complementary set that tells you how you're doing. None really stands alone.

207. Don't be afraid to collect bills.

208. Pay your bills, or at least let your vendors know when they will be paid. Make sure their expectations are always met.

209. If you're given the option of confronting someone with an issue that's driving you crazy or letting it fester, confront the person.

210. When traveling, don't get in the habit of buying gifts everywhere you go. If you are somewhere and see a great gift, get it.

211. Data is always a very powerful impetus for making decisions.

212. Real employee involvement means that at least 10 percent of the workforce is engaged in meaningful activity related to organization change or improved operations.

213. Learn what the labor movement is all about, how it's changing, and what it means to your industry. Be unbiased as you learn.

214. Spend time understanding what "real work" is, like working on an assembly line or driving trucks. It will ground you in reality.

215. If your mother or father gets fired, write a nasty but rational letter to the president of the company.

216. While looking for a job, buy an answering machine and check your messages.

217. Incremental change should take weeks or months, not years.

218. Set up ground rules at planning or decision-making meetings and get everyone to agree. Spell out the behavior you're after. Some examples are:

- It's okay to fight, just "don't go to bed mad."

- Attack issues, not individuals.

- Stick to the agenda.

- Think creatively.

- Work toward solutions and results, not processes.

- Look toward making things better. Don't dwell in the past.

219. Talk to people on planes. (I keep changing my mind on this one.)

220. All organizations have a mission and a culture. The question is, Is it the right one? You don't need to spend a lot of time creating one.

221. If people won't work with you, or you never get picked for projects, you had better ask why. People learn valuable lessons when choosing up sides on the playground.

222. If you can help it, don't fly on weekends for business.

223. Memorize your phone calling card number.

224. Write letters or send postcards (even if they're from hotels) home to your children. Have them start a collection.

225. Performance review systems and forms don't work. If you need to, create your own.

226. Ask a lot of questions about decision making like: Is there a decision that you want me to make? How do we make a decision on this? When can we expect a decision?

227. If you're in a job that requires paying attention to regulatory compliance issues, such as tax or employee benefits, make sure you pay attention.

228. Straight-legged pants (non-pleated) means you have an old suit.

229. New systems will probably not eliminate work or people. Chances are good that the volume of work will increase once customers know what a system can do.

230. Time the presentation of your business card so people will hold onto it and remember it. It's usually not smart to hand it over immediately upon meeting.

231. If you throw a company or departmental party and no one comes, you have a morale or teamwork problem.

232. Hospitals are to the 1990s what railroads were to the 1890s. It doesn't mean there will be jobs there. It does mean that there will be extraordinary changes there.

233. The most effective suggestion system is the one where the CEO puts a sign over his or her door that says "Suggestion Box."

234. Don't show any signs of vanity even if you are. A mirror in the office is always in poor taste.

235. Learn what vesting means, how it applies to you, and when it will kick in.

236. When using an overhead projector, don't cover part of the slide. It's annoying, and people will be wondering what's under the black part. If you want suspense, use more than one slide.

237. The most important variables in performance reviews are your own ability to keep track of what you do and whether or not your supervisor likes you.

238. One thing you learn in college is: "If it's free, eat it or drink it." Don't use that rule at work or at conferences. You're not at college anymore.

239. Learn the difference between running a meeting and leading a group.

240. Organization change happens faster when choices are limited in number—or eliminated.

241. If senior management doesn't see a need for change, it won't happen or the attempts will be so painful that people will leave rather than keep on trying.

242. Morale is a catch-all symptom that means the organization is in bad shape—but morale is a symptom, not a problem. If there are "morale problems," look for what's causing them, such as lack of security, pay cuts, or a jerk senior-management team.

243. Organization change will not occur unless employees believe it is in their best interest.

244. If there's not a strategy, it can't be implemented.

245. When the word "required" is used, it will generate a different response than when a decision is based on a little input.

246. In any decision-making process there is a finite number of options, usually not more than five. They include: (1) Keeping things the way they are; and (5) Changing everything in a dramatic way. Which really leaves three options. Pick one and move forward.

247. Never have more than three people from your side in a sales call.

248. Adding more systems to a bad system makes a big bad system.

249. Reengineering work that no one should be doing wastes time and makes everyone frustrated.

250. When giving a talk, think of what people will remember. And that's only one or two things.

251. Résumé gimmicks rarely work. Don't glue pennies to your résumé or design it so that it folds into a cube.

252. Don't take temp jobs for more than three months unless you love it or it may lead into a job with benefits.

253. "This is a gray area," means we don't know, but we're hoping the other department will handle it.

254. Changing the work area always gets attention—good or bad.

255.

When you hear . . .	What it could mean . . .
Strategic Consulting	Eliminate corporate staff and decentralize the business.
Benefits Choices	It's going to be more expensive with a higher deductible.
Get employees involved	Hold an employee meeting to tell them what is going to happen to them.

256. Customer-service improvement initiatives should receive more attention than others.

257. Launching a utilization study means we've been doing this for years, but we never counted it.

258. Empowerment and involvement usually mean the same thing to companies, but they shouldn't mean the same to you. Empowered means you should be able to make decisions and have sign-off authority, no matter what your level. Involved means you'll be kept posted and probably put on teams, but may or may not be involved in decisions.

259. The most devastating word for job seekers is "unfortunately."

260. When productivity improvements leave you with nothing to do, find something fast that will grow revenue.

261. Pessimistic futurists are to be ignored.

262. The more your goal is to make life simple, the more it will go in the opposite direction.

263. Never sit in the dunk tank at the company picnic.

264. The higher the level of a manager referring a job candidate, the worse the candidate.

265. Cross-training always creates good opportunities—learn what it is and get it.

266. Don't wear turquoise pinkie rings.

267. Ignore any new fashion trend with its roots in the 1960s or 1970s.

268. Use the phrase "value-added" infrequently.

269. Develop curiosity and gather information about topics such as retirement and saving for college educations.

270. If you call the "Help Line" or "Help Desk," be nice to the people who answer the phone. It's an impossible job.

271. Being mean to service people, especially restaurant or hotel help, only embarrasses those around you—and rarely changes anything.

272. Keep your résumé updated.

273. If you alphabetize your tapes and CDs, remember that most of the world doesn't work that way.

274. If you write a memo to someone above you in the chain of command, do not send blind copies to anyone.

275. The photos in recruiting brochures never reflect real life on the job.

276. No matter how late you work, always arrive at work on time.

277. Understand the concept before spending lots of time on the mechanics and the details.

278. Check your voice mail frequently, even when traveling.

279. The important things are rarely written down.

280. Data is not inherently good or bad, but accurate data that drives decisions quickly is good.

281. An abundance of worker's compensation issues either means people are getting hurt or people don't want to go back—or both.

282. Employees don't need incentives to work safely.

283. "Career path" implies a well-worn route. The truth is that you make your own way running around the organizational bushes and brambles.

284. The true sign of being overworked is not overtime. It's stress.

285. Never expect employees to be truly honest in front of their boss.

286. Write things down in your calendar—even if you're sure you'll remember.

287. Occasionally ask yourself, "If I had to bill my time, would anyone pay for it?"

288. Always allow more time than you think to get to the airport. Especially in New York City.

289. The sun will always shine on your computer screen when you don't want it to.

290. There is no such thing as a probationary period. We're all on probation, every day.

291. Don't make 900-number calls from your boss's phone.

292. After particularly hard days, go home and build forts out of blankets with your children.

293. There is a gap between the marks that customers will give you and what employees will give you. Employees know what the possibilities are. Narrow the gap.

294. Don't sponsor expensive golf tournaments for customers at the same time you're raising prices.

295. The sales people should be the organizational cheerleaders and optimists. If they're not, make some changes.

296. Listen to field people.

297. Technology eventually evens out. Compete on service and talented people.

298. When you say or hear, "We're doing the right things; it just takes time," rejoice and speed things up.

299. Turnover is contagious.

300. Never answer a question with the word, "whatever."

301. Read the article in the *Wall Street Journal* on the front of Section B, lower left-hand corner, every day.

302. Verify the pronunciation of people's names.

303. Buy building blocks for your children and other toys that they can pass along to their children.

304. Being late for meetings is rude.

305. Have family meetings, especially before vacations or during crises.

306. Make sure your children know you are proud of them.

307. Be proud of your children, no matter what.

308. If, in front of your boss, you pull the door when the handle says push, just keep going.

309. At no time, under any circumstances, use a toothpick in public.

310. Applying fingernail polish while on an airplane is like flossing your teeth on an airplane. Some things should be done in private.

311. Borrow David Letterman's "Top 10 List" concept when giving presentations.

312. Ask a college student what is hip. Then be yourself.

313. Telling ethnic or gay/lesbian jokes may not get you fired, but it could. At the very least, you'll be labeled something that will hurt your career. Don't do it.

314. Store your college textbooks with your parents until they announce they're moving. Then throw them away.

315. When consultants are brought in, someone believes that costs are too high.

316. Stay in touch with your best friends from high school and college.

317. Spend Sunday mornings in quiet time.

318. "Find a passion and follow it" is all the career advice you'll ever need.

319. A split-second is the time between when you stub your toe and when it hurts. That's how long it takes to make a decision.

320. Regardless of your line of work, never ask, "Are we a profession?"

321. Be wary of those whose hair
is never mussed up.

322. Ask yourself, "What can I be an expert in?" and become one.

323. If your expertise coincides with the company mission, Hallelujah.

324. Presentations must tell a story even if they are filled with data.

325. Every once in a while, discuss the size of leprechauns and elves and whether or not you believe in them with your staff.

326. Never show a chart or diagram that people can't read in a presentation.

327. Bite off more than you can chew and chew it well.

328. Learn to send faxes from remote locations like airports, hotels, and your mother's house.

329. Wear Kelly green pants only to play golf.

330. Since we may be stuck wearing blue or gray suits or other conservative clothes, wear ties or accessories with an attitude.

331. Facilitate or lead meetings with a point of view about what needs to be done and how we get there. Be open to changing your mind.

332. The hiring process always takes longer than both seekers and employers want.

333. Landing a job is as much a function of timing as it is qualifications.

334. Your children can probably help you define what you do. . . . "My Dad helps companies work better." (Management consultant.) "My Mom helps companies get known." (Public relations.)

335. If you take the last cup of coffee, at least take the pot off the burner. Make someone's life easier.

336. Get professional shoe shines in airports and hotels.

337. If, during a presentation, everyone has left the room, or everyone is talking, take a break.

338. We all know how we do in job interviews, sales calls, and meetings. Reconcile your expectations accordingly.

339. The purpose of a résumé is only to get an interview. Don't have ulcers over the color of the paper, print size, or margins. Those issues are not that important to the real people who can hire you.

340. Be sure you have some talent before you volunteer for the company talent show.

341. While looking for a job, never answer the telephone early in the morning by saying, "This better be good."

342. Never tell the person who is interviewing you for a job that he or she looks like a golden retriever.

343. There are never as many staff jobs as there are line jobs. Remember that landing a job is often a function of probability.

344. If you're in a tense business situation, ask yourself, "What would Bob Newhart do?"

345. The purpose of the staff is to make the line's jobs easier.

346. Maintain a keen sense of humor when looking for a job. You'll need it.

347. Always be prepared with an appropriate toast and pre-meal blessing—and remember the words to the national anthem.

348. Don't expect people to be 100 percent candid when the protagonists are present. Third parties always become the messengers.

349. Your personal life will always suffer if things are not going well at work. Minimize that impact.

350. Lava lamps should not be kept on your desk—or at least don't plug them in.

351. Working in a cubicle is more the norm than not. Don't let not having an office spoil your time at work.

352. Go to the company picnic—but don't stay long.

353. The sentence, "Salary is secondary to challenge, growth, and opportunity," is one of the great lies.

354. In outdoor team-building exercises, don't let your team pull your jeans down while using you as a ladder to climb over the "wall."

355. Harassment is an act of misconduct. Do it, and you'll lose your job. It's not whether—it's when.

356. Learn the difference between harassment and a very demanding boss.

357. Suspenders, bow ties, short skirts, cowboy boots, and big jewelry will always attract attention. Don't wear them if you don't want attention.

358. Don't answer the phone by barking out your last name.

359. After a hard project or long trip that has had you distracted, send flowers to your spouse or partner.

360. Congratulate people who accomplish something, even if you haven't seen or talked to them in years.

361. Always keep the ball in their court.

362. When everyone "games" the numbers, change the measurement system to change the games.

363. There's nothing to do about airplane delays. Don't get upset—use the time productively.

364. Learn the difference between groupware and Tupperware. Both are very useful.

365. When you make a change and in response you hear phrases like, "Same old horses, same old glue," or, "We're rearranging the deck chairs on the *Titanic*," then you didn't change enough.

366. Use "ASAP" only when it's urgent.

367. Convert training into experience as soon as possible.

368. Never give a bad reference. Simply decline to comment if there's nothing good to say.

369. When someone says, "This job wouldn't be bad if it weren't for the people and the telephone," don't put him or her in customer service.

370. When requested to attend a meeting at 4:30 on Friday, and bring your badge and keys with you, don't go.

371. At the end of a great week, when you get in the car, put in the long-version tape of "Louie, Louie" and play it as loud as it will go.

Epilogue

The hunt for lessons "Too Simple Not To Know" continues. We are constantly seeking those "bullets" that will allow others to avoid mistakes and be more successful. If you have a contribution to make and it appears in future books, you will receive full acknowledgment in the next book. Send your aphorisms to:

Richard A. Moran, Ph.D.
c/o Box 29–134
San Francisco, CA 94129-0134

About the Author

Lois Teuta Photography

Richard A. Moran is the National Director of Organization Change for Price Waterhouse. He has worked in all types of organizations worldwide, from Apple Computer to Zurich Insurance. Moran helps organizations implement their strategies by keeping management focused and by getting lots of help from employees. He is the author of *Never Confuse a Memo with Reality*. In addition, he is coauthor of the 1993 landmark study, *Postcards from Employees*, which captured the perceptions of over 50,000 employees regarding their organizations and management as well as customer service and other work-related areas. He has been featured on CNN, National Public Radio, UPI, and other media on workplace and employee issues. Moran lives with his family in San Francisco.